WE CELEBRATE YOUR DECISION TO FOLLOW CHRIST!

First Steps

Copyright © 2023 Jakob Barrientos Ministries

All rights reserved.

ISBN: 9798737548827

DEDICATION

This book is dedicated to Jesus. It is only by His shed blood and incredible grace that we have the joy of walking with Him.

CONTENTS

1	First Steps	1
2	The Great Exchange	3
3	Deal With the Sin	5
4	The Bible	9
5	Prayer	13
6	Be Baptized	17
7	Holy Spirit	22
8	Witness	25
9	Find a Local Church	27
10	Why is Church Important?	30

FIRST STEPS

Dear Friend,

I rejoice with you over your decision to get right with God! You have taken the most important first step in a wonderful relationship with God. You may be making this decision for the first time in your life. If so, you have made the greatest decision of your life. The Bible says that *"whosoever calls on the name of the Lord shall be saved"* (Acts 2:21 NKJV). Rest assured, long before you made the choice to follow Jesus, He has been pursuing you! He wants to be your Savior, King, and very closest friend.

Maybe you consider yourself a prodigal. At one time, you walked with the Lord, but at some point, you decided to walk away and do your own thing. It could have been sin that took you further from God than you ever intended to go. Maybe the circumstances of life caused you to stop pursuing the Lord. There are many reasons we can drift away from God, but the important thing is that **today** you are making the decision to go after Him! Don't let the devil speak to you for one second saying, you've sinned too greatly, or forfeited salvation forever. Remember the prodigal son in Luke 15? He intentionally left his fathers house to go live a life of sin and rebellion. He ran far from home and even squandered the gift and inheritance that

First Steps

His father had given him. There was a moment when the son realized how horrible his life was without the blessing and favor of his father. When he decided to return home, he thought he may have to be a servant of the father. Instead, the father celebrated the return of his son. This is a picture of how God feels when his sons or daughters decide to come back to Him. He is celebrating your decision to come home!

Possibly you are an individual that has attended church, done the religious thing, but you realize that you are not right with God. You may realize that you know how to play church, but may be lacking a personal, intimate relationship with Jesus Christ. You are not alone. Jesus taught that there will be some on judgment day that miss heaven, even though they preach, pray, and even see miracles. The problem is they did not have a personal relationship with Jesus (Matt 7:21-23).

No matter what category you fall into, the important thing is that you have decided to get right with God and stay right with Him! As you read the pages of this book you will clearly see the next steps you are to take as you grow into your relationship with God.

Many Blessings,

Jakob Barrientos

THE GREAT EXCHANGE

Therefore, if anyone is in Christ, he is a new creation; old things have passed away; behold, all things have become new.
2nd Corinthians 5:17

If you have ever questioned the love of God, you only need to consider the cross of Jesus Christ. The Bible teaches that we have all sinned. Everyone has fallen short of God's high and holy standard (Romans 3:23). We all need forgiveness. Jesus loves you so much that he was willing to take your sin and punishment and receive it upon Himself. Not only that, but He takes His sinless, perfect life, and credits it to you. So, God The Father sees your sin applied to the cross, and He sees the perfect life of Jesus applied to your life. This is what we call "The Great Exchange" (2nd Corinthians 5:21). Your sin, for His righteousness. It is not a very fair trade if you think about it. But Jesus loves you so much he was willing to bear your punishment so you could be forgiven.

First Steps

How amazing that we have been given a clean slate! A new beginning! Now we get the opportunity to live a life that honors God. Be like Paul who said, *"...this one thing I do, forgetting those things which are behind, and reaching forward to those things which are ahead, I press toward the goal for the prize of the high calling of God in Christ Jesus"* (Philippians 3:13-14 NKJV).

First Steps

Deal with the Sin!

What is Sin? There is so much confusion around right and wrong. Today many trying to re-define right and wrong. There is a message that is being pushed that says if we make statements about sin or morality we are being hateful or judgmental. Everyone doing what is right in their own eyes (Proverbs 26:12). While there are many differing opinions about what is right and wrong, the Bible is very clear about sin. This Biblical standard is what God is judging our lives by.

Simply put, **sin is anything Jesus would not do**. Did you know that Jesus faced the same temptations that we do? In every way that you and I can be tempted, Jesus was tempted. But the Bible says that Jesus never sinned! Hebrews tells us that we, *"do not have a high priest* (Jesus) *who cannot sympathize with our weaknesses, but One who has been tempted in all things as we are, yet without sin."* (Hebrews 4:15 NASB). Jesus did not just come to save us **in** our sins, but it was prophesied that He would be the one to save us **from** our sins (Matthew 1:21). The Bible also teaches us that there is a way to face temptation without sinning just like Jesus did.

> *To this you were called, because Christ suffered for you, leaving you an example, that you should follow in his steps. "He committed no sin, and no deceit was found in his mouth." When they hurled their insults at him, he did not retaliate; when he suffered, he made no threats. Instead, he entrusted himself to him who judges justly. He himself bore our sins on his body on the tree, so that we might die to sins and live for righteousness; by his wounds you have been healed. For you were like sheep going astray, but now you have returned to the Shepherd and Overseer of your souls*
> 1 Peter 2:21-25 NIV

Jesus knew how serious sin was, which is why He was willing to suffer and die to free us from the punishment and bondage of sin.

Sin will enslave you: Jesus said, *"I tell you the truth, everyone who sins is a slave to sin"* (John 8:34 NIV)

Sin will destroy you: *"For the wages of sin is death; but the gift of God is eternal life through Jesus Christ our Lord"* (Romans 6:23 KJV)

First Steps

Sin separates you from God: *"But your iniquities have made a separation between you and your God, and your sins have hidden His face from you, so that He does not hear"* (Isaiah 59:2 NASB)

I would encourage you to pray and ask the Lord to help you do some house cleaning. I often say that its like breaking up with the devil. If you have ever had a breakup in your life, you know, if you keep the articles of affection, your heart will be reminded of that person you are tying to move on from. Their memory will keep you from moving on in life. It is the same with the devil. We need to break up with the devil and get rid of the articles of affection (sin). This is the only way we can enter into a right relationship with God.

If you ask the Lord, He will lead you. Remember, we are talking about walking with Jesus. This is a relational thing. As you go about your day, invite Jesus to be with you. You will notice at different times He may put His finger on an issue and let you know that something grieves Him. Be obedient! When you are listening to music, watching a movie, or spending time with certain people, pay attention to the presence of God. Is He with you, or do you feel His presence leave?

You do not need to find a copy of the 10 commandments to post on the wall to remember

First Steps

what you are allowed to do now that you are a Christian. The Bible says that God will write His law in our hearts and mind (Hebrews 10:16). Invite God to speak to your heart and to show you the things that cause Him to come near and the things that push Him away.

First Steps

The Bible

Reading the Bible should become a daily practice. While preachers and teachers and other books are beneficial, there is no substitute for The Bible. The Word of God is alive! It is the best way to get a clear picture of God's heart and His will for your life. You may have tried to pick up a Bible in the past and been confused or found it to be cold. Something happens when you come to faith in Jesus and are born again. The Holy Spirit helps to bring understanding to you. The Bible teaches that The Holy Spirit becomes a teacher and helper to us (John 14:26). There will be moments that you are reading the Bible, and something speaks straight to your heart. This is one of God's ways of communicating with His children.

The psalmist David spoke about the value of the word of God, *"I seek you with all my heart; do not let me stray from your commands. I have hidden your word in my heart that I might not sin against you. Praise be to you, O LORD; teach me your decrees"* (Psalm 119:10-12 NIV). And, *"Your word is a lamp to my feet and a light to my path"* (Psalm 119:105 KJV).

First Steps

The Apostle Paul wrote to his son in the faith, *"All Scripture is God-breathed and is useful for teaching, rebuking, correcting and training in righteousness, so that the man of God may be thoroughly equipped for every good work"* (2 Timothy 3:16-17 NIV).

There are many versions of the Bible today. We have computer programs and phone apps that make the Word of God more accessible today than any other time in history. People often ask which version of the Bible they should use. My typical response to that question is, "The one that you will read!"

Find a translation of the Bible that you can understand. The Bible was originally written in Hebrew and Greek. Most today do not read those languages. This is why we have different translations. You will notice that I have used several different translations in this book, and personally I use several translations in my own study times.

There are several versions of the Bible that were translated <u>word-for-word</u>. This means a team of translators would look at the original language (Greek or Hebrew), and find the closest word in the English language. The King James (KJV), New King James (NKJV), Amplified (AMP) and the English Standard Version (ESV) were all translated in this way. These are all great translations.

First Steps

Other versions of the Bible were translated <u>thought-for-thought</u>. There are a lot of rhymes, wordplay, and cultural references that are in scripture that are sometimes missed in a word-for-word translation. So, some teams came together to translate a paragraph or sentence from the original language, trying to capture the original thought. The New International Version (NIV) and The New Living Translation (NLT) are a couple examples of thought-for-thought translations that I would recommend.

Recently, there have been a few Bibles that have been released that fall into a third category: <u>Paraphrase Bibles</u>. Instead of a team of educated translators working together on a project, typically one individual will take scripture and express it in their own words, or as they understand it. The Message Bible, and The Passion Translation are two popular examples of Paraphrase Bibles. These can be beneficial as an addition to your library, but I would not recommend them as your Bible for daily reading. Just like hearing a preacher is not a substitute for reading the Bible, reading a paraphrase Bible is not a substitute for reading an actual translation of the Bible.

If you are beginning to read the Bible for the first time, I would encourage you to start with one of the New Testament Gospels (Matthew, Mark, Luke, and

First Steps

John). These books include the teaching and ministry of Jesus which is the centerpiece of the entire Bible. Reading the Psalms and Proverbs daily is recommended. I would not read the Old Testament (Genesis-Malachi) until after you have completed the New Testament (Matthew-Revelation).

First Steps

Prayer

Prayer is simply talking to God. You have asked Jesus to forgive you, come into your heart, and be your best friend. How often do you talk to your best friend? People often ask, "How often should I pray" or "How much do I need to pray?" Imagine if you treated your friend or your spouse that way. "How much do I really need to talk to them?" If you approach your friendships or marriage in that way, you are headed for trouble!

We should consider our time talking to God as the highest privilege. It truly is not difficult. In fact, in Matthew 6 Jesus rebuked some of the religious of the day for praying while using high and lofty speech. God does not speak King James Old English either. Talk to Him! In the morning say, "Good morning, Jesus! What are we going to do today?"

As with any conversation, it is a two-way dialogue. Talk to God about everything. Share your dreams, your struggles, and your victories. But be sure to take

First Steps

time to quiet yourself and listen as well. You will be amazed how often God will speak if you simply give Him a little quiet time.

You may feel unworthy to come to God in the place of prayer, but the Bible is clear: Once the blood of Jesus has cleansed your life, you can come before God with confidence!

> *Let us therefore come boldly unto the throne of grace, that we may obtain mercy, and find grace to help in time of need*
> Hebrews 4:16 KJV

Not only is God your helper, but Jesus said we can call on God as a Father. What a joy! We are received, not as slaves to a master, but as sons and daughters in a loving relationship with a Father.

The Bible has much to teach us about prayer. In fact, you will notice that Jesus never even taught His disciples how to preach, how to work miracles, or how to cast out demons. He did, however, teach them how to pray. This is because all other ministry flows from the place of prayer.

> *In the morning, O LORD, you hear my voice; in the morning I lay my requests before you and wait in expectation.*
> Psalm 5:3 NIV

First Steps

Evening, and morning, and at noon, will I pray, and cry aloud: and he shall hear my voice.
Psalm 55:17 KJV

Now it came to pass in those days that He went out to the mountain to pray, and continued all night in prayer to God.
Luke 6:12 NKJV

Pray without ceasing. In every thing give thanks: for this is the will of God in Christ Jesus concerning you.
1 Thessalonians 5:17-18 KJV

Jesus told the disciples, *"And when you are praying, do not use meaningless repetition, as the Gentiles do, for they suppose that they will be heard for their many words. Therefore do not be like them; for your Father knows what you need, before you ask Him"*
Matthew 6:7-8 NASB

"He shall call upon me, and I will answer him: I will be with him in trouble; I will deliver him, and honor him"
Psalm 91:15 KJV

Take time, every day, to get with God in the place of prayer. Talk to Him as you go about your day-to-

First Steps

day life. Include Him in everything! Also, be sure to take time to get in a private place here you can shut out the business and noise of life and really listen for His voice.

First Steps

Be Baptized

Did you know that before the word "baptism" was a spiritual term, it was a cooking term? You can trace the origins back to the Greek's dunking meat in wine or other substances as a marinade. Probably the most accurate example is the idea of a cucumber. When you take a cucumber and immerse (baptize) it in a mixture of vinegar, salt, and other spices, after some time it will begin to absorb the nutrients, flavor, and characteristics of the mixture it was immersed in. When you go back after several days, you will see that what is drawn out of that jar is no longer a cucumber, but it is now a pickle!

This is an accurate picture of what happens when we are baptized! You are immersed into the body of Jesus Christ. This is not just a religious ceremony or ritual. We believe that when you are received into the body of Christ, you literally begin to absorb the nature, characteristics, and power of God. You are no longer the old, sinful, broken person you were. Now you are a cleansed, renewed, saint of God!

First Steps

Baptism in the Bible can mean a few different things. You are baptized into the body of Christ. You are to be baptized in water. And, there is the baptism of the Holy Spirit.

Go therefore and make disciples of all the nations, baptizing them in the name of the Father and of the Son and of the Holy Spirit.
Matthew 28:19 NKJV

Baptism into Christ's body takes place the moment you are born again. The Holy Spirit has been working on you, drawing you to Jesus. There was a moment where your heart was opened, and you decided to accept Him as your Lord and Savior. At that moment, the Holy Spirit took up residence in you. This is what happened in John 20:22 when "*Jesus breathed on them, and said to them, 'Receive the Holy Spirit'*". At the same time, you were received into the Body of Jesus Christ.

You became filled with the Spirit of Life, rather than the spirit of death (Romans 8:1-2). In a certain sense, the Holy Spirit baptized you into Jesus Christ and His body.

Jesus answered, "Most assuredly, I say to you, unless one is born of water and the Spirit, he cannot enter the kingdom of God."

First Steps

John 3:5 NKJV

Baptism in water is an outward expression of your obedience to follow Jesus in His death, burial, and resurrection. It is like a wedding ceremony. If you are married, I am sure you told your spouse you love them privately before you expressed that on a stage in front of witnesses. In the same way, water baptism is you expressing publicly the love that you have already expressed for God privately. This the moment where you declare to the world where you stand, and that you are in a faithful, committed relationship to the Lord.

The immersion in water is a picture of your being united in the death of Christ. Because of His death, your sin is washed away. As you go under the water, it is a picture of being united with Christ in His burial. You are buried with Christ in Baptism (Romans 6:4). Being raised up out of the water is the picture of you being united with the resurrection life of Jesus.

"Therefore we are buried with him by baptism into death: that like as Christ was raised up from the dead by the glory of the Father, even so we should walk in newness of life."
Romans 6:4 KJV

I would encourage you to seek baptism by immersion (not sprinkled, but totally dunked) from a qualified Pastor or Minister. It was one of the few commands that Jesus left us with. If you are returning to the Lord after a long season away, I would encourage you to be baptized again. I would remind you of the earlier illustration I made about marriage. Imagine if you had walked away from your marriage for several years. If you were to return to your spouse, would you feel the need to rededicate that marriage? Most likely! It is the same way with the Lord. We do not need to be re-baptized after every sin, anymore than we need to be remarried after every argument. However, if there was an extended season you were not in relationship with Jesus, I would encourage you to consider baptism once again.

Baptism in the Holy Spirit. You will notice when you are received into the body of Christ, Holy Spirit was the one who did the work of bringing you to Jesus. John the Baptist said of Jesus, *"I baptized you with water; but He will baptize you with the Holy Spirit"* (Mark 1:8 NASB). After you are baptized into Christ and His body, His desire is to then baptize you into the Holy Spirit.

The Holy Spirit filled you the moment you believed but being baptized in the Holy Spirit is the Holy Spirit on you and all around you.

And I [Jesus] *will ask the Father, and He will*

give you another Counselor to be with you forever – the Spirit of Truth. The world cannot accept him, because it neither sees him nor knows him. But you know him, for he lives with you and will be in you.
John 14:16-17 NIV

The baptism in the Holy Spirit is available to any born-again believer. This amazing gift from God empowers us to grow properly as a child of God. Let us learn more about the Holy Spirit and His active role in our lives.

First Steps

Holy Spirit

Holy Spirit is the manifest presence of God on the earth. As Jesus was approaching the time where he would ascend to Heaven, He promised to send another helper. A Counselor who would be with us forever.

But the Helper, the Holy Spirit, whom the Father will send in My name, He will teach you all things, and bring to your remembrance all things that I said to you.
John 14:26 NKJV

Beyond being a constant help, part of the role of the Holy Spirit is to give us the strength and power we need to fulfill the call God has on our lives.

But you shall receive power when the Holy Spirit has come upon you; and you shall be witnesses to Me in Jerusalem, and in all Judea and Samaria, and to the end of the earth.
Acts 1:8 NKJV

First Steps

And suddenly there came a sound from heaven, as of a rushing mighty wind, and it filled the whole house where they were sitting. Then there appeared to them divided tongues, as of fire, and one sat upon each of them. And they were all filled with the Holy Spirit and began to speak with other tongues, and the Spirit gave them utterance.
Acts 2:2-4 NKJV

And when they had prayed, the place was shaken where they were assembled together; and they were all filled with the Holy Spirit, and they spoke the word of God with boldness
Acts 4:31 KJV

Jesus, before beginning His public ministry was empowered by the Holy Spirit. At the time of His baptism (Matthew 3:13) He was not only immersed in water, but the Bible records that as He was coming out of the water, the Holy Spirit descended and rested upon Him. This is very important, because in the next chapter we see a moment when Satan himself came to tempt Jesus, but the Bible says that Jesus overcame the devil, he was led by the Spirit (Matthew 4:1), and was operating in the power of the Holy Spirit (Luke 4:14).

If Jesus saw the need to be filled and empowered by the Holy Spirit, how much more do you suppose

First Steps

we need to be filled and empowered?

How are you baptized in the Holy Spirit? The Bible gives quite a few examples. The first thing you need to do is simply ask God to baptize you with His Spirit! God desires to give you the Holy Spirit.

> *If you then, being evil, know how to give good gifts to your children, how much more will your heavenly Father give the Holy Spirit to those who ask Him!*
> Luke 11:13 NKJV

There are other moments in the Bible where it is recorded that people were baptized in the Holy Spirit when another Spirit filled believer laid their hands upon them. One instance of this is recorded in Acts 8:14-19.

Of course, there was the famous account in Acts 2. There was a group of 120 individuals waiting and praying in an upper room. God visited that small assembly in a powerful way, and everyone in the room was filled with the Holy Spirit and began to speak in other tongues.

I would encourage you to begin to seek out the baptism of the Holy Spirit. Pray for it in your personal prayer time. Get plugged into a spirit filled church that takes the time to pray in this way. Get involved in corporate prayer and Bible study with people that will believe with you for the baptism of the Holy Spirit.

Witness

Let your light so shine before men, that they may see your good works, and glorify your Father which is in heaven
Matthew 5:16 NKJV

One of the particularly important steps that I would encourage you to take is to begin to share your faith with others. You may be thinking, "I just got right with God! You are saying I should begin sharing my faith already?" Yes! Absolutely!

As you begin to read through the gospels you will read some incredible encounters that Jesus had with individuals. There was a heavily demonized man that was chained up and considered to be crazy and without hope. Jesus instructed him to go and share with others about all the things God had done for him! There was a woman that was a 5-time adulterer and living unmarried with a man. Of course, we know about the disciples who came from all sorts of sinful backgrounds. But one thing all of these have in common… After they encountered Jesus, He immediately instructed them to begin to share about the wonderful things God had done for them.

Don't think that you need to get some formal education or need to complete a 3-year program before you are qualified to share with someone. I would encourage you to go to the people that are close to you, and begin to share with them, in your own words, what God has done for you.

Your testimony is so powerful! And in my experience, it is the people that are just getting right with God that have the greatest success in witnessing. Possibly this is because they still have many close relationships with people that are still in the lifestyle they are coming out of. Possibly it's because of the transformation that others begin to witness. I think its also significant that most people who are just getting right with God remember what its like to be lost and hopeless. They remember what it feels like to experience the love, and forgiveness of Jesus for the first time.

I would encourage you to keep those memories fresh in your mind. Reflect on the cross of Jesus Christ. Consider how much He loves you, and what it felt like when you realized your sins were forgiven and you had received a new life!

First Steps

Find a Local Church

The next thing that is especially important for every believer is to get connected to a local body of believers. With technology today, it has become extremely easy to hear preaching and worship through social media, podcasts, television, and other platforms. While these outlets can be wonderful, none of them fulfill what God intended for us, personally, to receive and be a part of in a local body.

Something that is extremely important when searching for a church knowing what they believe. The 3 most important questions you need to know about the church are:

1. What do they believe about the Bible?
2. What do they believe about God?
3. What do they believe about the Holy Spirit?

What do they believe about the Bible? We have

already covered the importance of the Bible. It is important to hear what a church believes about the Bible. Do they believe in the whole Bible? Do they preach the whole Bible? Some would argue that the Bible has error or is just one of many spiritual books. Some would place the book of Mormon, or the Quran on the same level as the Bible. Others teach that the Bible is not relevant and needs to be modified to fit a contemporary audience.

Avoid a church that does not preach the Bible! If a church or pastor does not believe that the Bible is the Inspired word of God, you can be sure that the foundation of the entire church is faulty.

There are 3 "I's" that should be believed about the Bible:

Inspired. We believe that the Bible is inspired and authored by God. Of course, God spoke through people, but we believe that God didn't just inspire the thoughts of the writers, but the very words of scripture.

Inerrant. We believe there is not error in the Bible. When God inspired the authors to write the scripture, He used people of vastly different backgrounds and styles to clearly express His message exactly the way He intended it.

Infallible. The Bible is incapable of error and will accomplish exactly what God intends for it to. The Bible clearly and accurately expresses the heart of God and His will for us.

What do they believe about God? Do they believe in the Trinity? The idea that we believe in One God, eternally existent, in three persons: The Father, Son, and Holy Spirit.

The Bible teaches that there is only one true God, The God, and Father of our Lord Jesus Christ. The shed blood of Jesus is the only way we can be forgiven of our sins and saved. There is no alternative path, faith, or religion that will save your soul.

What do they believe about the Holy Spirit? Another major factor in the church you choose to be a part of is the ongoing ministry of the Holy Spirit. Simply put, do they believe God is still working in the earth today through the Holy Spirit? I also covered this in an earlier section. Get involved with a church that believes in the power of prayer and will contend for a move of God today!

First Steps

Why is Church Important?

Jesus desired for His Body (The Church) to be in fellowship. Although we all look vastly different, have different gifts, and different areas of ministry, we are all a part of the Body of Christ. Keep in mind that we are all people in process, and God is still working in all of us (Philippians 1:6)!

There is no perfect church. I heard one pastor say, "If you ever find the perfect church, don't go there, because you will ruin it." True! The fact is, because the church is made up of imperfect people, the church will be imperfect. Our goal is to give and receive love from one another.

And let us consider one another in order to stir up love and good works, not forsaking the assembling of ourselves together, as is the manner of some, but exhorting one another, and so much the more as you see the Day approaching.

First Steps

Hebrews 10:24-25 NKJV

Jesus made it clear, that His method to destroy the works of the devil on the earth was to build a mighty church that hell itself would not be able to overcome (Matthew 16:18). It is also important to note that every time we see a mighty move of the Spirit, an outbreak of miracles, or many people coming to faith in the Bible, it was always when people were **assembled together**.

In Acts Chapter 2, there was a group of 120, and the Bible says they were **assembled together** (Acts 2:1). As they sought the Lord, God visited them in a dramatic way. There was a sound like a tornado that hit the area. They were all filled with the Holy Spirit, received tongues of fire, and 3,000 were saved in one moment!

In Acts 4, there was a group of believers and the Bible says they were **assembled together** (Acts 4:24). When they prayed in that moment, the Bible says the entire building was shaken by the power of God, and they were filled with the Holy Spirit, empowered to boldly preach the word of God.

In Acts 5, there was a group of believers and the Bible says they were **assembled together** (Acts 5:12). As they were together, God worked miracles, signs, and wonders among the people.

First Steps

You will see the same thing over and over and over again in the Bible. In fact, as you read the book of Acts, you will notice that on nearly every occasion you saw miracles, healing, the casting out of demons, or any mighty move of God, you will always see a phrase like "They were assembled together", or "They were together in one accord" or "in the place they assembled".

There is something powerful that happens when we assemble with other believers to worship, pray, and hear the teaching and preaching of God's word.

Get connected to a local church. I always encourage people who do not know what church they should attend: <u>Find the most on fire man or woman of God that you know, and go to church where they go to church</u>. If that church preaches the Bible, preaches Jesus as the way to salvation, and believes God is still working miracles today, dig roots in that church. Find a place where you can serve and so something for the Lord.

The church is the best place for you to grow in your relationship with the Lord. A good pastor will do what they can to equip you for the call that God has placed on your life (Ephesians 4:11-12).

I'm so thankful that you have chosen to take your

first steps with the Lord. It is the best decision you will ever make. If you take the principles that I've expressed in this book, you will find that you are already well on your way to growing in a strong relationship with God!

ABOUT THE AUTHOR

Jakob Barrientos has a burning passion to see the lost come to Jesus and to see those bruised and bound by the enemy healed and set free! After being arrested on drug charges, and God miraculously raising him up from a drug overdose he's been on a mission to see God touch the lives of those who desperately need Jesus.

Jakob and Leah are both graduates of Christ for the Nations. Jakob spent several years traveling and ministering alongside his mentor, the late revivalist and evangelist, Steve Hill. For seven years they served as Senior Pastors of a growing and fruitful church in Central Illinois. Jakob and Leah have led and taught evangelism teams at Christ for the Nations and traveled extensively as evangelists both locally and internationally. Jakob served as the staff evangelist of Trinity Church in Cedar Hill under the leadership of Pastor Jim Hennesy.

In 2017 Jakob and Leah joined the staff of King's

First Steps

Cathedral and Chapels under the leadership of Dr. James Marocco.

Today, they are on assignment to plant churches on the Island of Hawaii (The Big Island). They are pioneering a new work in Kailua-Kona. Jakob and Leah live in Kona with their two amazing children, Moriah and Gabriel.

Made in the USA
Monee, IL
19 October 2024